A Friend is a Special Treasure

by Sophia Bedford-Pierce

Photographs by Solomon M. Skolnick,
hand-painted by Jill Sabella
Designed by Mullen & Katz

PETER PAUPER PRESS, INC.
WHITE PLAINS, NEW YORK

The publisher wishes to thank our stars:
Sarah Beilenson, Brielle Burns, Kristen da Costa, Gina Gill,
Thaddeus Logan III, Sophia Skolnick, and Kelly Tacon.

A Friend is a Special Treasure

Introduction

Grandma Sophie's legacy took many forms. Amongst the treasures that she bestowed on me were a hammer (and of course a bag of nails), a tape measure, a needle, a thimble, instructions on how to craft a dozen types of knots, gardening gloves, a love of hats, and her diaries. She always said (and meant it) that "you can't do the right job without the right tools." She also believed that "you can never have enough hats" (and she meant that too). Of all the treasures that she gave to me, however, the most precious was her ability to teach by example.

I marveled then, as I do now, at Grandma Sophie's sense of self-worth and her ability to appreciate the worth of others. She knew how to make each of her friends shine in their own light. Grandma really believed that every person was special and every friendship was to be treasured.

I often re-read Sophie's diaries. And as I do, the voice of a happy and wise woman who loved the fullness of life speaks to me again and again. "May all your friendships be good ones," she would say. What Grandma Sophie gave to me I gladly share with you.

S. B-P.

Friendship

is a

great

adventure.

Laughter
helps
a friendship
last.

Treasure
friendship
like a
bouquet of
flowers.

Choose
a friend as you
would a book,
by what's
inside.

Friends often heal the battered spirit.

Friends
remain friends
wherever
they may go.

Plant
the seeds of
friendship.

Have a
friend
(or two)
over for tea.

Walk
beside me
and be
my friend.

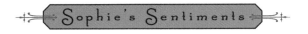

A friend
is a friend,

rain

or shine.

Friends
enjoy
sharing their
interests.

Friendships
bear
sweet fruit.

A friend's
company is
the sound of
music.

A friend
knows
how to
communicate.

Friends
never let you
get too big
for your
own shoes.

Friends
light up
your life.

Friends enjoy
exploring
the unknown.

Friendship
is the gift
of a
lifetime.

The flower
of friendship
is always
in bloom.

A cheerful friend,
like a sunny day,
sheds joy and
lightness on
all who are near.

True
friends
stand
together.

The End.